30 Days

To Overcome

Fear of Missing Out (FOMO)

A Mindfulness Program with a Touch of Humor

Harper Daniels

Copyright © JV 2020

This book is meant to be a guide only, and does not guarantee specific results. If the lessons and exercises in this book are followed, change can occur for certain people. Results vary from person to person; some people may not need to complete the thirty days to experience change, but it's encouraged that the entire program be read completely through at least once.

The last half of the book consists of blank note pages that the reader can use in conjunction with the exercises for each day. The reader is encouraged to utilize the note pages; though it's not necessary.

Give the gift of mindfulness. See similar guides at www.30DaysNow.com if you wish to purchase a book for a loved one. **See the disclosure below.**

Disclosure (Shared Lessons and Exercises):
Keep in mind that our mindfulness guides share the same lessons and exercises, so there is no need to purchase more than one book; unless you are sharing with a group or giving the guides as gifts. Our mindfulness guides are created for various topics; however, they utilize the same lessons and exercises, so please be aware of this before purchasing. For example, *30 Days to Overcome FOMO* will mostly have the same lessons and exercises as *30 Days to Reduce Anxiety* and so forth. By reading just one of our guides, you'll be able to apply the same lessons and exercises to multiple areas of your life.

Enjoy your journey of self-discovery!

Contents

Preface……………………………………………………….4

Day 1……………………………………………………...…7
Day 2………………………………………………………...8
Day 3………………………………………………………...9
Day 4……………………………………………………….10
Day 5……………………………………………………….11
Day 6……………………………………………………….12
Day 7……………………………………………………….13
Day 8……………………………………………………….14
Day 9……………………………………………………….15
Day 10……………………………………………………...16
Day 11……………………………………………………...17
Day 12……………………………………………………...18
Day 13……………………………………………………...19
Day 14……………………………………………………...20
Day 15……………………………………………………...21
Day 16……………………………………………………...22
Day 17……………………………………………………...23
Day 18……………………………………………………...24
Day 19……………………………………………………...25
Day 20……………………………………………………...26
Day 21……………………………………………………...27
Day 22……………………………………………………...28
Day 23……………………………………………………...29
Day 24……………………………………………………...30
Day 25……………………………………………………...31
Day 26……………………………………………………...32
Day 27……………………………………………………...33
Day 28……………………………………………………...34
Day 29……………………………………………………...35
Day 30……………………………………………………...36

Conclusion………………………………………………….37
Note Pages……………………………………Begins on 38

Preface

It seems as though everyone has experienced FOMO (*Fear of Missing Out*) at one point or another. What about you? What is it that you're afraid of missing, either in the present or the future? Are you concerned about missing an event, a business opportunity, a relationship, a travel destination, a living experience, a higher education, or starting a family? FOMO can be experienced with regard to almost anything. Whatever experience you're afraid of missing out on, it's not worth the fear, worry, and anxiety. This mindfulness program will help you drop an unhealthy attachment to FOMO, so that you can start living a happy and fulfilling life in the present moment.

With the prevalence of social media, FOMO is on the rise at an extraordinary pace. Online pictures and news feeds are sending messages about the latest events, newest restaurants, most popular trends, recent tech products, hottest travel destinations, and so forth. Businesses, organizations, and influencers are using FOMO to drive revenue; it's no secret. Marketers hope that you experience FOMO continuously, so that you'll fall in line and buy whatever they're advertising, at a significant price. As you'll discover throughout this mindfulness program, that price is your present moment happiness. The time to awaken and drop the fear is…now. There is no need for FOMO in your life.

For the purpose of this book, let's define *FOMO (Fear of Missing Out)* as: an attachment to the misperception that there are better experiences to be had, away from your present moment experience. If this definition appears too complex, you can define FOMO any way you wish - as long as you recognize it as an attachment to a false idea of experience and happiness. However you define FOMO, please understand that it's an attachment to a fear based illusion that you've been conditioned to accept and believe. You might even define FOMO as anything that encourages you to assert thoughts such as: *"I must be part of...,"* *"I must experience...,"* *"I must have...,"* or *"I must try...to feel fulfilled and happy."*

The following pages involve a 30 day mindfulness program made up of lessons and exercises to help you overcome patterns of thinking, feelings, and attachments that have kept you stuck in a state of FOMO. Though these lessons and exercises can be applied to any unhealthy reliance, this program will focus specifically on the misconception of FOMO.

For some readers, they'll overcome the old reliance quickly and will drop the pernicious thoughts and dependency in no time; and for others, they'll overcome the fear slowly and gradually. In either case, if you stick with the program, you'll start to witness the effects of the perceived fear weaken. Please don't judge your progress in the program, as this isn't a competition and there isn't a goal you must attain. Let the debilitating thoughts, feelings, habits, and attachment simply drop as you work through the exercises and lessons.

It's not necessary to complete the program's days in order, nor should you be religious about completing them successfully. There is no such thing as a successful completion of this program. The bottom line is to observe and awaken, and that cannot be obtained through success, force, pressure, struggle, or competition. Simply relax, follow the program, and FOMO will loosen.

You'll also notice that mindfulness, silence, and stillness are a regular discipline for each day in the program.

Because you've been influenced by a dependency based society that demands instant gratification, silence and stillness may seem nearly impossible for you to practice. For this reason, we'll incorporate this discipline from the outset. A quiet and still mind is an incredibly powerful resource, but one that requires daily maintenance.

It should also be noted that you're not required to ignore or fight FOMO during the program; however, if you've already dropped it, then do not pick it up again. The point being: by practicing the following exercises and lessons in the days to come, you won't even need willpower to move on from FOMO – it'll just happen.

You'll need about 15-30 minutes per day for the program; but feel free to spend more time if needed. The amount of time doesn't matter, as long as you're in an environment that allows you to concentrate without distraction. Also to be mentioned, the last 30 pages of this book are clear note pages that correspond to the 30 days. It's encouraged that you write down any thoughts, insights, adaptations, lessons, mantras, etc, on those blank pages. The note pages can also be used to rip out and take with you. Feel free to use them as you wish.

One last thing: If you're like most people, you might be dependent on caffeine, alcohol, or sugar to some extent. If you are, do your best to lessen the consumption of these substances over the next 30 days. It's not necessary that you abstain, but can you cut consumption of these substances in half, or more? It's important that your mind is sober and your body relaxed to make the most of these exercises and lessons.

Let's get started.

Day 1

Exercise:

Find a place without distraction, and turn off all electronics. Sit with your back straight, kneel, or lie on a hard surface (not bed) and remain in silence for 10 minutes.

During these 10 minutes, take deep and focused breaths and hold them for a few seconds each. Exhale slowly. Listen intently to your breathing. Don't try to change it – simply listen, and feel the air go in and out.

*When you're ready, repeat the mantra: "**Be still. Be silent.**" Repeat this slowly multiple times out loud as well as quietly. You might experience boredom or anxiety, but continue repeating the mantra regardless. Repeat it until you're calm and focused. You can continue the deep breathing during the mantra, or take deep breaths during pauses. Don't rush.*

Each of the 30 days will have this time of silence, focused breathing, and a mantra. Except for this page, the end of each day will remind you of the minutes you are to spend in silence and focused breathing; and will also have a mantra for you to practice. You can repeat the mantras during your times of silence and focused breathing, or following. Remember, there is no right or wrong way to do this.

Adverse thoughts and feelings want to fight; in fact, they're energized by fighting. Instead of fighting FOMO, meet it with silence and observation. Let the exercises and lessons in this program guide you.

Day 2

Exercise:

Ponder this question: Can you remember a point in your life when you didn't experience a fear of missing out?

Writing is extremely beneficial to the mind; especially when pondering. Write down your thoughts about this particular question. If your mind drifts, then write whatever thoughts emerge. It's okay if you have nothing to write, but ponder the question regardless.

Were you able to remember a period in your life when you weren't experiencing FOMO? If you're like many people, you may have to return to memories of childhood to determine that period. It's not uncommon for a person to experience fear of missing out at an early age, and continue experiencing it throughout life.

Recognize that FOMO is a learned attachment with roots. However, it can be dropped quickly and completely; and you have the capability to drop it. In other words, you are not controlled, identified, or dominated by a learned misconception of what does, or does not, lead to happiness.

*10 minutes of silence and focused breathing. Repeat the mantra: "***Drop. Unlearn. Discover.***"

Day 3

Exercise:

On a sheet of paper (any size) write down all the internal lies that you regularly hear about yourself – i.e. within your mind.

Now, tear the paper into multiple pieces, and throw away.

It's common to have an internal voice (or voices) within your mind, playing a record of lies over and over. We eventually begin to accept these lies and let them impact our growth and happiness. Most people you see on a daily basis have these recurring internal voices; and most people are oblivious to them – sort of like white noise. This isn't a mental illness, but a way in which the mind works. We all experience these internal quiet voices whispering untruths about our being. These lies are nothing to fear, but they need to be observed. Writing them down can help you observe and become aware of their deceptions.

The power of silence, focused breathing, and mantras, which you have been practicing, is to draw out the lies. Let them manifest, and observe them. Common internal lies include: *"You're a failure if you don't do that," "You'll screw up your life if you don't experience this," "You'll always be subpar," "Your best isn't enough; you'll just fail," "You'll make a fool of yourself; so don't even try,"* and so on. These thoughts are not part of you; however, the deception is to make you believe they are. The stresses, concerns, and anxieties of FOMO can implant many of these lies clandestinely.

*10 minutes of silence and focused breathing. Repeat the mantra: **"Thoughts are only thoughts - nothing more."**

Day 4

Exercise:

Observe your body. Observe how it feels, moves, and reacts. More direction is explained below.

If you're currently experiencing FOMO about something, observe your body movements, sounds, sensations, and breaths during the fear experience. Do your eyes dim or widen? Are your breaths shallow or deep? How is your posture? Are your shoulders tense or relaxed? Is your voice low or high pitched? Try to observe everything about your body while in the grips of FOMO. Be aware of its affect on your body.

If you are not experiencing FOMO today, then continue with the 10 minutes of silence and focused breathing, but get in touch with your body. A good way to do this is by touching each body part and saying its name, leaving your hand on the part for a few seconds and feeling its texture and warmth. Start with your head: place your hand on your head and say, "*I am touching my head.*" And then work your way down to your shoulders, arms, stomach, legs, knees, and feet. Focus your attention on one body part at a time. Say its name and describe what you are touching.

The point of this exercise is to bring you into awareness, where you can awaken to FOMO's impact on your body. In the end, *you* are not your body with or without FOMO.

*10 minutes of silence and focused breathing. Repeat the mantra: "*I am not my body.*"

Day 5

Exercise:

On a piece of paper (any size) write down the goals that you've been striving to achieve – i.e. the goals that you believe will bring you fulfillment. For example: a new job, a house in a nice neighborhood, traveling the world, a business, a family, new friends, a degree or certification, building a network, reaching a net worth of a million dollars, etc.

Now, tear up the paper into multiple pieces and throw away.

Goals can be very helpful and useful if they're not obsessed over. However, in the modern world people develop a reliance on goals. Think about all the times you've said something like, "*I need to get that*," "*I must reach this*," "*I'll do anything to accomplish that*", etc. It's often the case that people spend more time worrying about their goals, than freely doing something in the present moment to reach them. Plus, the goal in itself is fleeting, while the journey in the present moment is real and lasting.

The habit of thinking that goals must be met, or else failure ensues, is subtly fixed to dependencies. What goals are you holding onto tightly? Which goals are conjoined with the FOMO that you may be experiencing? In other words, what goal does FOMO serve?

*10 minutes of silence and focused breathing. Repeat the mantra: **"My happiness does not depend on meeting a goal. I'm happy now."**

Day 6

Exercise:

Find a hard object that you can hold in the palm of your hand (such as a stone, ball, or bottle). With either hand, grip this object tightly and squeeze it as hard as you can. Squeeze it forcefully until you can't hold on to it any longer. Drop the object when ready.

If you could continue squeezing that object forever, perhaps you would; but your muscles and nerves can only endure for so long. At some point, you simply and quickly release the grip and drop the object. There isn't a process to the drop; it just happens when your body says that's enough. The release happens naturally without effort.

Letting go of an unhealthy dependency, habit, thought pattern, addiction, emotion, or behavior can be that easy. Letting go can be as natural and guilt free as dropping the object you were gripping on to so tightly in this exercise; so, take a lesson from your body's experience. When it's time to let go, then let go. The time to let go is always now. Just let the drop happen.

FOMO can have a whimsical hold on your life – it's an illusion and false perception. Let it go; and live your life in the present moment, free and happy. Surround yourself with reminders to experience the present moment.

*10 minutes of silence and focused breathing. Repeat the mantra: **"Letting go is natural. I can let go, here and now."**

Day 7

Exercise:

Today, look for the color blue in your surrounding environment. If possible, spend the entire day looking for the color blue in the places you go. Whether you're doing this exercise in a bedroom, office, classroom, outside, or while traveling, look for the color blue in all things that surround you. If you think you'll forget to do this throughout the entire day, spend at least 20 focused minutes practicing this exercise at some point.

Focused attention is something that must be practiced - it doesn't come easy in our rapid paced society. Instead of encouraging us to focus and observe, the modern world encourages us to rush and get things done.

Searching for a color or shape helps to slow down our accelerated and cyclical thought patterns, and reminds us that there's more to the world than the chaotic thoughts we collectively and daily experience. By searching for the color blue, your mind can escape the fictitious grip of anxiety, lust, desire, depression, worry, fear, or any other potent emotion. When you experience FOMO, are you aware of the colors around you? Most likely not.

FOMO functions to distract your conscience from present reality. Look for the color blue today, and awaken to life in the present moment.

*10 minutes of silence and focused breathing. Repeat the mantra: *"I am focused, here and now."*

Day 8

Exercise:

Stand in front of a doorway, with the door open. Close your eyes, and take a deep breath. With eyes closed and holding your breath, step through the doorway. Once you have stepped through completely, open your eyes and exhale.

Doorways offer great lessons for practicing mindfulness and observation. How often do you rush through doors without paying attention to the change of environment? We don't often pay attention or appreciate the transition; we simply rush through unaware that our perspective has changed. This isn't a bad thing; in fact, it's great that we don't stall in front of doorways, too afraid to enter the next environment. At the beginning of this exercise you were in a particular place, and then you stepped through a doorway into a completely different setting. You made a transition without worry or concern, and very naturally.

When it comes to physical doorways, we rarely stop and worry about the change of environment – we just walk through and accept the new experience. You can apply this same lesson to decisions that have you stressed, anxious, or worried regarding FOMO. Step through the feelings and accept the changes; but try to step through aware and grateful. There will always be a doorway leading to new experiences. When you drop the misconceptions of FOMO, new doorways will be present.

*10 minutes of silence and focused breathing. Repeat the mantra: **"I accept change with awareness and gratitude."**

Day 9

Exercise:

Take a piece of paper (any size, but large enough to draw on); with a pen, scribble a random line with your eyes closed. Don't lift your pen from the paper; keep it as one messy scribble. Only spend two or three seconds doing this.

Now, with your eyes open and seeing what your scribble looks like, make it into an actual image of something. Work with the scribble to make something noticeable.

What did you make out of your scribble: an animal, house, drifting balloon, kite, a person, a scenario, an entire scene with many things, etc?

This is one of my favorite exercises. It's a lesson that teaches that the scribbles and confusions we experience in life can be changed and formed with a new perspective. Life is all about perspective. How do you perceive scribble, mess, chaos, clutter, disarray, and confusion in your life experience? Do you know that you can perceive it differently starting now?

In silence, stillness, and with an open mind, take a look at any scribbles that you may be experiencing in life. If you observe long enough, without judgment or concern, you will gain a new perspective. Don't let FOMO determine the perspective of your scribbles.

*10 minutes of silence and focused breathing. Repeat the mantra: **"I am not confused. My perception can always change in the present moment."**

Day 10

Exercise:

Focus on a natural object or scene for 10 minutes, without distraction and in silence.

Focusing on a natural object for an extended period of time is an ancient practice. How often have you stopped to observe something objectively for more than 10 minutes? When was the last time you've quietly watched a sunset, sunrise, tree sway in the wind, bird chirping, clouds passing or expanding, or just a rock? That might sound boring, but this practice is very liberating. If you look at anything long enough, you start to see it from a different perspective. As easy as this exercise sounds, it's not – try it out, and see how long you can observe without thoughts impeding the practice.

Watching a bird feed may be more interesting than watching an immobile rock; but I encourage you to start with an immobile object, such as a stone or piece of wood. During this process thoughts will emerge – observe the thoughts and let them pass. Don't attach a goal or benchmark of success to this exercise; just observe an object.

The goal and purpose of FOMO is to hypnotize you with a false narrative; stealing your attention from the present moment. Wake up to what's around you in the present.

*10 minutes of silence and focused breathing. Repeat the mantra: **"Be focused. Observe. Be present."**

Day 11

Exercise:

Go for a mindfulness walk for at least 10 minutes. Focus on each step. Feel the steps: the feel of your feet hitting the ground, your heel rolling forward, your toes, the bend of your knees, your hips working to balance your posture, the swinging of your arms, etc. Don't rush; go slow. Focus on your breathing as well. Get in tune with your body. Pay attention to your physical senses throughout the walk. Focus – don't listen to music or be distracted.

Human beings have always used walking as a naturally restorative exercise. There is something about walking, and focusing on the walk, that calms the mind and soul. The longer one walks, the more relaxed one feels.

Any moment is a good time to walk and experience your inner and outer environment. During long walks, thoughts will emerge that will allow you to consciously observe them. Let the thoughts pass; you may even have emotions that emerge, observe those and let them pass as well. Focusing on your steps will help you clear the mind of clutter. Walking in the early morning and at dusk is especially beneficial.

A 20 minute walk brings more comfort, stillness, peace, focus, and awareness than hundreds of hours in the grips of FOMO. Walk every day, as much as you can.

*10 minutes of silence and focused breathing. Repeat the mantra: "*I am relaxed. I am at peace.*"*

Day 12

Exercise:

Find an object that you can break: an egg, a drinking glass, a pencil...anything. In a safe place, break the object of your choice, and be especially careful if it's glass or something sharp.

Don't clean up the pieces immediately, observe the mess and let the pieces sit for at least a few minutes.

Did you break the object, or did I break the object by directing you to break it? And if you believe it was only you who broke the object, did the object allow you to break it? This isn't an exercise meant to release frustration or stress. The purpose of this lesson is to show you that you're not 100% responsible for your perceived chaos, mess, loss, failure, or broken pieces. The lie of FOMO is that you're responsible for broken, failed, and missed opportunities and experiences. Don't believe the deception of FOMO.

Destruction happens in the present moment, and that's OK. We spend so much time and energy worrying about goals, relationships, jobs, situations, the future, and other things breaking into pieces. And when that happens, we tend to blame ourselves or others, because that's what we've been taught to do. Allow breaking to happen; and observe the pieces as well as your reaction to the destruction.

*10 minutes of silence and focused breathing. Repeat the mantra: **"I cannot harm or break the present moment."**

Day 13

Exercise:

Hold a smile for 5 minutes. You don't need to do this exercise in front of a mirror; but feel free to do so if you wish. You can even do this exercise during the 10 minutes of silence and focused breathing. While holding your smile, take a moment and feel your face; actually touch the smile and the curvature of your lips and cheek bones.

Have you ever behaved a certain way and then saw your mood change immediately? Physical exercise, such as running and weightlifting, does this for many people. Certain forms of yoga have also been used by people to change their moods. The point is: changing your behavior not only impacts other people, but can also impact your perception of yourself.

You'll notice that while you're smiling during this exercise, you may experience certain emotions. You might feel silly, embarrassed, stupid, funny, weird, or whatever. Continue smiling regardless. In fact, if you're still experiencing FOMO at this point, smile while you're in the grips of it – hold the smile as long as you can; set a reminder alarm if needed. As always, observe your thoughts while you're smiling; observe the thoughts as if they're clouds passing by in a bright blue sky.

Smiling causes an authentic reaction in our bodies and minds that is essentially good. The present moment enjoys a nice smile. So practice holding that smile.

*10 minutes of silence and focused breathing. Repeat the mantra: *"**Happiness is now. I am happy.**"*

Day 14

Exercise:

Most food products have a "Nutritious Facts" label that will tell you the percentage of fat, cholesterol, sodium, carbohydrates, protein, and other important nutritious content in the product. Let's make one for your experience.

On a sheet of paper, write down the words: happiness, stress, anxiety, worry, anger, and depression. Feel free to add other words that describe emotions and feelings that you may regularly experience. Now, next to each word write down the percentages that best represent their measure in your life. There is no right or wrong for this exercise; the point is to become keenly aware of what emotions and feelings you are experiencing more often than others. If you write 70% depression, that is not "bad". Simply be honest with the percentages; recognize them.

Which emotions received the highest percentages? Which received the lowest? Remember, you are not your emotions or feelings; however, you do experience emotions and feelings, and some of them will be experienced more than others, especially during and after episodes of FOMO. If you are experiencing adverse emotions more often than positive ones, then don't let that bother you. Whatever emotion you experience in the present moment, observe it and let it pass. For the negative emotions that come regularly, examine them and let them fade. Observation is the key to understanding.

*10 minutes of silence and focused breathing. Repeat the mantra: **"I am not ruled by emotion. I am here and now."**

Day 15

Exercise:

Choose a song to listen to carefully. You can choose the song from your music collection; or simply turn on the radio and wait for a song to play.

While listening to the song, don't listen to the notes, beats, voice, or rhythm; instead, listen for the silence between sounds. Listen for the stops, pauses, and absence of sound between notes. Listen for the silence in the song.

Have you ever realized that your favorite songs would not exist without silence? Every note, rhythm, beat, and voice needs a moment of silence to manifest – even if that moment exists in a millisecond. Without silence, there would be no noise, yet alone music. This isn't to say that noise and silence are in conflict; quite the opposite actually. Sounds and silence are complementary. So, were you able to hear the silence within the song? Practice this repeatedly whenever you listen to music. Listen for the silence that allows the music to endure.

Similarly, we need silence to let the rhythm of life manifest. Unfortunately, this has become a struggle for many people, because we live in an unbalanced world that encourages sound over silence. Don't listen to the noise that accompanies FOMO, and don't fear silence. Silence is a powerful remedy. Practice remaining in silence daily; you'll start to hear and see new and wonderful things.

*10 minutes of silence and focused breathing. Repeat the mantra: **"Be silent. Listen. Be silent."**

Day 16

Exercise:

Lay down on the floor (not on a bed or couch), with your back straight and your arms at your side. Close your eyes.

Now, imagine yourself in a coffin or under the ground. If this depresses you, do it regardless. With your eyes closed, imagine not being able to open them ever again; also imagine not being able to move your body or speaking ever again. Stay in this position for 10 minutes, or as long as you can.

If this seems gothic or dark, that's only your learned perception of the death experience. There's an ancient teaching that says the way to enlightenment is through a keen awareness of death. The person who is daily reminded that the body will die, and faces this fact head on with a clear mind and acceptance, has nothing to lose and is truly free to live in the present moment. The question isn't whether or not your body will die (because it surely will); the more important question is: will you live before death?

Will you truly live before your body dies? The present moment is the only thing you'll always experience. Instead of fearing a pending death, accept it and be thankful for the present moment, and live in it without FOMO!

*15 minutes of silence and focused breathing. Repeat the mantra: **"My body will age and pass, but I will always be present - free from fear."**

Day 17

Exercise:

Turn off your cell phone, or put it in airplane mode, for at least 1 hour, and observe the thoughts you experience. If you don't have any major responsibilities this day, or if you have all you need and don't require the phone, then turn off your cell phone for 12 hours. This exercise works best if you can go 24 hours without your cell phone activated; but go no less than 1 hour. If there are people who are immediately dependent on you, send them a text saying that you'll be unavailable, and then turn off your phone.

Like never before we live in a world with a plethora of distractions. All of these distractions fight for our attention, because money is behind the scenes. Every business is wondering how they can break your distraction from one thing so that you can be distracted by their thing – whether that thing is a product or service. It's a constant war for your attention, response, and reaction. Whoever can hold your attention the longest, wins the battle; but whoever can make you dependent, wins the war. Social media has become an important weapon in this war of distraction; and the smartphone is the gateway. It's time to power off.

When you turned off your phone, what thoughts emerged? Were you concerned that you weren't receiving certain messages, missing out on the latest news, skipping great deals, etc? FOMO wants you to stay distracted; so do everything you can to lessen outside distractions.

*15 minutes of silence and focused breathing. Repeat the mantra: *"I am not distracted. I am present, here, and now."*

Day 18

Exercise:

Say the words "Guilt", "Shame", and "Regret" 10 times to yourself out loud. Don't rush. Pause between each repetition. For the pause, you can take a deep breath. Your eyes can remain open or closed. Again, don't rush - say the words slowly and observe any thoughts, feelings, or images that emerge internally.

Now, say these words again 10 times, but with a smile.

What futile credence we give words such as Guilt, Shame and Regret. We use these words on ourselves as well as others; they become regular vocabulary for our internal recurring voices. And in the end, they're mere words that hold no power. What would these words be without a facial expression, tone, inflection, or emphasis?

When you said these three specific words, what thoughts came to mind, what did you feel, and was there a reaction in your body? If there is a reaction, such as shortness of breath or a frown, people tend to interpret it as sadness; but this reaction is a learned behavior. We've been taught to feel and think a certain way with regard to guilt, shame, and regret. The truth is: these words mean nothing.

FOMO, like most adverse attachments and misperceptions, flourishes on these three words and the learned reactions they produce. But see them for what they are...mere words with no power.

*15 minutes of silence and focused breathing. Repeat the mantra: **"I am not Guilt, Shame, or Regret."**

Day 19

Exercise:

Go out and buy a small trash can. You should be able to find one cheaply. If you don't have the funds for this exercise, you can use an empty box or container; however, a small trash can works better for its symbolism.

Designate this specific trash can your "concerns and worries can" (or use any title you wish) – some people benefit from writing this label directly onto the can.

Now, write down (on scraps of paper or whatever paper you wish to use) any concerns, worries, and adverse thoughts that you may be experiencing today, and throw them into the can. Try to practice this every day: quickly write down worries, concerns, and negative thoughts, and then throw them into the can. It may be beneficial to have a supply of scrap paper near the can for easy access.

This exercise may seem simple, but let's go beyond throwing your written concerns, worries, and thoughts away. Designate a few times during the week for sifting through the can and taking out random worries and concerns from days prior – just reach in and pull some out. Observe them, but don't judge yourself. This is a great exercise to learn your negative thought patterns and the lies that grip your conscience. If you stick with this practice, you may gain a deeper understanding and realization into the dependencies, habits, thought patterns, and feelings that may have you gripped by FOMO.

*15 minutes of silence and focused breathing. Repeat the mantra: **"There is nothing to worry about. All is well."**

Day 20

Exercise:

Choose a physical symbol that will remind you to observe and be aware in the present moment. Try to choose something from nature, or that is made of natural material.

The object you choose can be anything, but it's best if it's something that you can enjoy looking at and touching. For example, many walkers and hikers will find a unique rock small enough to carry in their hands. A stone, necklace, bracelet, seashell, cedar block, coin…anything will do, as long as you enjoy it and you can dedicate it as a tool for remembrance.

Another cunning trick of FOMO is to confuse the mind into forgetting you're part of the external natural world. The misperceptions and lies of FOMO prey on, manipulate, and influence the imagination. Thus, you're taken out of physical reality. By having a symbol of remembrance, you can reconnect with the present moment. This symbol isn't meant to be an idol, god, or icon. Don't think too deeply into this. The symbol is simply a tool to help you remember where you are in the here and now. As long as you're aware of the present, you'll have no desire to return to the hallucination that accompanies FOMO.

*15 minutes of silence and focused breathing. Repeat the mantra: "**All is well. Here and now, all is well.**"

Day 21

Exercise:

Find a coin. While standing, flip the coin and let it land wherever. If it lands with the head side up, spin around to the right until you come back to your original place; if it lands tail side up, spin around to the left until you come back to your original place. Again, head side up, spin to the right; tail side up, spin to the left – doing a full circle until you return to your original standing position.

In which direction did you spin? In this exercise you left the direction of your movement completely up to the flip, the coin, and gravity. When you spun, you experienced a specific visual perception of the environment that you would not have had from spinning in the opposite direction. But, you returned to the original position regardless, full circle.

The experience would have been different if you spun to the opposite side; and if you repeat this exercise multiple times, your experiences in the same direction will be different as well. The point being: it doesn't matter what direction you go in or what you experience in life; you'll always return to the present moment; so the time to be awake, aware, and happy is always now.

You will always have access to the present moment, so enjoy being here and now. FOMO doesn't command the present. *Fear of missing out* doesn't exist; it's an illusion.

*15 minutes of silence and focused breathing. Repeat the mantra: "**The direction does not matter. I am always here and now, in the present moment.**"

Day 22

Exercise:

On a sheet of paper (one that you can easily save and return to later) make a list of hobbies that you've had in the past but have neglected, and also make a list of hobbies that you would like to start in the future.

From these lists choose one hobby from the past and one new hobby that you'd like to start. Focus only on these two – the old hobby and the new one. Make this a priority.

How often have you said, or have heard other people say, *"I wish I had the time."* You do have the time. You just choose to think of time in the way that you've been taught to perceive it. If your life depended on it, you would certainly make the time if needed.

In fact, time is a manmade construct - don't ever forget that. There is only the present moment. Past and future are not here and now. We spend far too much time thinking about time. How many of your recurrent inner thoughts involve questions such as, *"When will that ever happen?" "When will I ever change?" "Why did that have to happen?" "If the past were different, life would be better."* These are lies that only eat into the present moment, and infect our modern world.

Ruminating thoughts brought on by FOMO can occupy and steal the present moment; and that moment could be used to pursue hobbies that magnify your happiness.

*15 minutes of silence and focused breathing. Repeat the mantra: **"The time is now. Happiness is present."**

Day 23

Exercise:

Pinch the skin on the back of your hand or forearm until there is discomfort and slight pain. It's not necessary to pinch hard enough to bruise yourself, just enough to feel a small burn.

Did I cause the pain by asking you to do this exercise? No; you caused this pain to yourself – think about this carefully. You even decided how much pain to give yourself, and when to relieve the pain. You can't blame me or anyone else for the pain you just experienced. You were solely responsible. You were also responsible for letting go.

This is easily understood with regard to physical pain, such as pinching oneself; however, we have a lot of difficulty understanding this lesson as it applies to adverse emotions and feelings. How often have you said, and have heard others say, *"He makes me so angry when..."*, *"I'm depressed because she..."*, or *"I'm so frustrated that they..."* No person ever makes you experience negative feelings. It's always you who are experiencing them; and then placing the blame on others. Essentially, you are emotionally pinching yourself and not letting go.

People go their entire lives without releasing the pinch. Instead of letting go, they scream at others, *"Release the pain! Let go! Fix this! Stop this! You're to blame!"* Wake up and see that you are solely responsible for letting go of the pain, and you can do it now. You can't blame anyone for the FOMO you experience; only you can let it go.

*15 minutes of silence and focused breathing. Repeat the mantra: *"I can release negative feelings, here and now."*

Day 24

Exercise:

Choose a book; perhaps one that you have at home that you haven't read in a while, or from the library. You can also use a long article for this exercise. It's best if you haven't read the book or article beforehand.

Now, instead of reading from the beginning; read the last chapter (or paragraph if it's an article) first.

Does this go against your conventional way of perceiving a story? Did you feel that it's pointless to even read the entire book, or article, since you're aware of its ending before reading the beginning? Just because you started at the end of the book doesn't impact the story; instead, it impacts your perception.

If you've been struggling with FOMO for a while; is it the beginning, middle, or end of your experience? This isn't to teach you that you can control the end or beginning of an experience; because you can't. The purpose is to show you that the present moment is all you'll ever need, and you can accept the end as the beginning and the beginning as the end, if that's your experience in the present moment. So, be open to perceive all things as they are now, with or without a beginning or end. In other words, be awake, don't worry, and be happy. FOMO is a misconception, illusion, and hypnotic state of thinking. It's not the beginning of an end. The time is always now.

*15 minutes of silence and focused breathing. Repeat the mantra: **"There is no end or beginning. Only now."**

Day 25

Exercise:

Write a letter or email to yourself. There is something about using pen and paper that is very effective when writing letters, but feel free to write an email if you wish. Don't send the letter or email, just write it and save it for a day – you can toss it out or delete it tomorrow.

Write anything that comes to mind: It can be advice you want to give yourself, a story from the past, random thoughts and feelings, frustrations and worries, things you're thankful for, etc. There is no right or wrong – write whatever comes to mind in the moment. Try to write at least two full paragraphs.

What was the theme and voice of your message? Was it a positive or negative tone? Were you advising yourself? Did you make any judgments about yourself? Did you start demanding that you should or should not do something? Was the letter full of gratitude? Was there anger and despair? Read the letter as if you were reading it from a friend – is it a letter that would upset you, or one that you would welcome with excitement and a smile?

Whatever you wrote is essentially being written on the tablet of your mind. This exercise is useful for getting to know the internal voice that we all have in our minds. It's an internal voice that can change for the better with observation, acceptance, and awareness. Be aware of your internal voice in the present moment, and how it responds to FOMO.

*15 minutes of silence and focused breathing. Repeat the mantra: "**I am not my internal voice. I am aware.**"

Day 26

Exercise:

Think of a major worry that consistently upsets you. On a sheet of paper, write down three worst case scenarios for that dominating concern. For example, if someone is persistently worried about failing a specific job, that individual can write as a worst case scenario, "I will do poorly at the job, and will be fired; leaving me homeless and broke." As mentioned, write down three worst case scenarios for your particular worry. You can even choose a worry related to FOMO.

Now, next to each of those three worst case scenarios write, "I accept this." You can either toss the paper or keep it.

Worry is an illness that goes untreated in most people, especially when experiencing FOMO. Think of worry like a cancer of the spirit; but few people know how to treat it effectively. One of the only ways to eradicate worry isn't to fight, ignore, or run from it; but to face it in the present moment and accept it for the illusion it is. You can never be worried about something happening in the present moment – that's impossible; you can only be worried about the future, which is always illusory.

Writing down your worries and worst case scenarios, if they ever do come true (which they rarely do), is a great way to draw those thoughts out of your mind and into the present moment, allowing you to face, accept, and observe them.

*15 minutes of silence and focused breathing. Repeat the mantra: **"Worries are not real. They are only thoughts."**

Day 27

Exercise:

Using objects that can stack (rocks, books, boxes, containers, pillows, etc), stack them slowly and carefully until they fall.

When the stack collapses, smile and laugh.

The lives of many people are spent stacking things for the goal of success, as defined by society. People stack possessions, knowledge, relationships, degrees, money, jobs, toys, businesses, experiences, etc. They stress, fight, fatigue, compete, become ill, and get anxious and depressed through the process of stacking; yet, few people have found happiness. Society tells us that if our stack is high and mighty, we'll have obtained success. What a deception. What are you stacking; or what do you feel compelled to stack?

Allow the stack to fall. This lesson is not encouraging complacency; but instead teaches that real, authentic, and fulfilling experiences can only happen apart from the stress and worry of stacking. When you stack, you're focused on the future and the perceived importance of the stack; and then you have to maintain that heap of nonsense, which requires a lot of anxiety and pressure. Focus on your experience in the present moment; and if the stack falls, then smile and laugh.

*15 minutes of silence and focused breathing. Repeat the mantra: **"I allow the stack to fall."**

Day 28

Exercise:

Imagine this scenario: It is 3:00 AM. You wake up and realize that your home is on fire. Everyone, except you, is out of the house. You realize that you only have a minute or less to get yourself out before everything is destroyed. You must act immediately.

With such a short amount of time, what do you grab to take with you?

Really consider this scenario; because it happens to people every day around the world. People are forced to leave their homes because of fire, flood, violence, and other uncontrollable factors. If this happened to you, what physical things would you grab and take in such a short window of time? Your cell phone, a piece of clothing, family pictures, computer, passport, specific files, a project, or nothing at all? Whatever you take within that moment will be the most meaningful objects to you. What does this tell you about your desires, attachments, concerns, needs, and habits?

Adverse misperceptions, such as FOMO, want to influence what we deem important and unimportant. Focus on the few, and present, things in your life that you know have true value. Whatever you're experiencing FOMO about, more than likely doesn't have true value in the present moment. Never allow FOMO to tell you that a physical possession is essential for your happiness.

*15 minutes of silence and focused breathing. Repeat the mantra: "*I am not my possessions. I am free from material things.*"*

Day 29

Exercise:

Make yourself laugh for 5 minutes. Don't stop laughing. You might feel strange, weird, embarrassed, or stupid...it doesn't matter, just laugh. Try to laugh alone and without the aid of a comedy or joke. If you don't know how to start, just start making the noises that typically accompany your laughter.

What feelings did you experience during this exercise? Many people report feeling embarrassed or goofy, which is great; however, most people also report a feeling of relief and buoyancy when they've completed this exercise.

Similar to holding a smile, laughing for 5 minutes is a fantastic way to come into present awareness. If you think about it, humor is necessary for life. How sad is the person who is unable to laugh at the experiences of life? After all, life is funny, even the dreadful and lousy experiences.

If you ever again experience adverse thoughts and feelings that accompany FOMO, simply laugh at them. Consider how crazy and frivolous it is to have a fear of missing out, and your reactions to it. FOMO really is a funny and absurd misperception. No other living thing on the planet gets bothered by a misconception of experience and happiness. The entire situation is comical. If you perceive FOMO for what it truly is - a fictitious, impractical, and frivolous idea – then it can be easily dropped. You must learn to laugh at it. Genuinely laugh FOMO away.

*15 minutes of silence and focused breathing. Repeat the mantra: *"**Life is wonderful, funny, and real.**"*

Day 30

Exercise:

Take a piece of paper (one that you can keep) and write down all that you are grateful for – these things don't have to be in any particular order of importance.

Next to each thing you list, write "Thank you."

The person who isn't thankful for all that life gives is typically quite miserable; and FOMO thrives on that negativity. The truly grateful person can let go of anything at anytime. A thankful person is always a happy person, so practice gratitude daily.

Have you ever heard anyone say, *"I'm so grateful for fear of missing out"*? Nobody is thankful for FOMO; which is a clear sign that it's an unhealthy misperception. However, a few people have learned to be thankful for the present moment experience.

Not only is it unhealthy, but an attachment to FOMO and its misperception of happiness discourages a grateful mind and soul. With only one life to live in the present moment, it's important to always emphasize a grateful heart. Spend time with people who are grateful, and do things that nourish a thankful heart in the present moment. Anything that encourages misery and fear isn't worth giving attention to. Be thankful, always.

*15 minutes of silence and focused breathing. Repeat the mantra: **"I am grateful. I am thankful."**

Conclusion

The exercises and lessons in this program taught and encouraged observation, awareness to your present moment experience, change of perception, and awakening to true happiness, which can only be found here and now. You were shown that your negative thoughts and feelings are not caused by FOMO, or any unhealthy misperception or reliance, but are solely within you and illusory; which means that you are capable of letting those thoughts and feelings pass and dropping the fear in the present moment.

As mentioned at the beginning, there were no goals or measures of success for this program. If you were hoping to find a reason to act on FOMO, then you may be spending too much time struggling and thinking about whatever it is you believe you're missing out on. This was not meant to be a struggle or competition, but a release.

Life is not meant to be spent dealing with the FOMO, or any type of unhealthy misperception. Wake up to the present moment and enjoy your present experience. If you've made it through the program, you are certainly more awakened than when you started; however, don't give up mindfully practicing observation of thoughts and feelings, stillness, silence, deep and focused breathing, allowing everything to pass, laughing, smiling, and being grateful.

Live wonderfully awakened and aware…with or without the fear of missing out.

Notes for Day 1

(Use the space below to write down thoughts, reminders, ideas, new mantras, revelations, lessons, modifications to the exercise, experiences, etc.)

Notes for Day 2

(Use the space below to write down thoughts, reminders, ideas, new mantras, revelations, lessons, modifications to the exercise, experiences, etc.)

Notes for Day 3

(Use the space below to write down thoughts, reminders, ideas, new mantras, revelations, lessons, modifications to the exercise, experiences, etc.)

Notes for Day 4

(Use the space below to write down thoughts, reminders, ideas, new mantras, revelations, lessons, modifications to the exercise, experiences, etc.)

Notes for Day 5

(Use the space below to write down thoughts, reminders, ideas, new mantras, revelations, lessons, modifications to the exercise, experiences, etc.)

Notes for Day 6

(Use the space below to write down thoughts, reminders, ideas, new mantras, revelations, lessons, modifications to the exercise, experiences, etc.)

Notes for Day 7

(Use the space below to write down thoughts, reminders, ideas, new mantras, revelations, lessons, modifications to the exercise, experiences, etc.)

Notes for Day 8

(Use the space below to write down thoughts, reminders, ideas, new mantras, revelations, lessons, modifications to the exercise, experiences, etc.)

Notes for Day 9

(Use the space below to write down thoughts, reminders, ideas, new mantras, revelations, lessons, modifications to the exercise, experiences, etc.)

Notes for Day 10

(Use the space below to write down thoughts, reminders, ideas, new mantras, revelations, lessons, modifications to the exercise, experiences, etc.)

Notes for Day 11

(Use the space below to write down thoughts, reminders, ideas, new mantras, revelations, lessons, modifications to the exercise, experiences, etc.)

Notes for Day 12

(Use the space below to write down thoughts, reminders, ideas, new mantras, revelations, lessons, modifications to the exercise, experiences, etc.)

Notes for Day 13

(Use the space below to write down thoughts, reminders, ideas, new mantras, revelations, lessons, modifications to the exercise, experiences, etc.)

Notes for Day 14

(Use the space below to write down thoughts, reminders, ideas, new mantras, revelations, lessons, modifications to the exercise, experiences, etc.)

Notes for Day 15

(Use the space below to write down thoughts, reminders, ideas, new mantras, revelations, lessons, modifications to the exercise, experiences, etc.)

Notes for Day 16

(Use the space below to write down thoughts, reminders, ideas, new mantras, revelations, lessons, modifications to the exercise, experiences, etc.)

Notes for Day 17

(Use the space below to write down thoughts, reminders, ideas, new mantras, revelations, lessons, modifications to the exercise, experiences, etc.)

Notes for Day 18

(Use the space below to write down thoughts, reminders, ideas, new mantras, revelations, lessons, modifications to the exercise, experiences, etc.)

Notes for Day 19

(Use the space below to write down thoughts, reminders, ideas, new mantras, revelations, lessons, modifications to the exercise, experiences, etc.)

Notes for Day 20

(Use the space below to write down thoughts, reminders, ideas, new mantras, revelations, lessons, modifications to the exercise, experiences, etc.)

Notes for Day 21

(Use the space below to write down thoughts, reminders, ideas, new mantras, revelations, lessons, modifications to the exercise, experiences, etc.)

Notes for Day 22

(Use the space below to write down thoughts, reminders, ideas, new mantras, revelations, lessons, modifications to the exercise, experiences, etc.)

Notes for Day 23

(Use the space below to write down thoughts, reminders, ideas, new mantras, revelations, lessons, modifications to the exercise, experiences, etc.)

Notes for Day 24

(Use the space below to write down thoughts, reminders, ideas, new mantras, revelations, lessons, modifications to the exercise, experiences, etc.)

Notes for Day 25

(Use the space below to write down thoughts, reminders, ideas, new mantras, revelations, lessons, modifications to the exercise, experiences, etc.)

Notes for Day 26

(Use the space below to write down thoughts, reminders, ideas, new mantras, revelations, lessons, modifications to the exercise, experiences, etc.)

Notes for Day 27

(Use the space below to write down thoughts, reminders, ideas, new mantras, revelations, lessons, modifications to the exercise, experiences, etc.)

Notes for Day 28

(Use the space below to write down thoughts, reminders, ideas, new mantras, revelations, lessons, modifications to the exercise, experiences, etc.)

Notes for Day 29

(Use the space below to write down thoughts, reminders, ideas, new mantras, revelations, lessons, modifications to the exercise, experiences, etc.)

Notes for Day 30

(Use the space below to write down thoughts, reminders, ideas, new mantras, revelations, lessons, modifications to the exercise, experiences, etc.)

Printed in Poland
by Amazon Fulfillment
Poland Sp. z o.o., Wrocław